CRYPTOCURRENCY

The Crash Course To Learn About Investing And Trading Cryptocurrencies Including Bitcoin, Ethereum, Monero, Zcash And More

Adrian McNulty

DEUXIEME PARTIE

Exercices & Apprentissages

« La théorie, c'est quand on sait tout et que rien ne fonctionne. La pratique, c'est quand tout fonctionne et que personne ne sait pourquoi. Ici, nous avons réuni théorie et pratique : Rien ne fonctionne... et personne ne sait pourquoi ! »

Albert Einstein

© Copyright 2018 by Adrian McNulty - All rights reserved.

It is not legal to reproduce, duplicate, or transmit any part of this document in either electronic means or in printed format. Recording of this publication is strictly prohibited.

Table of Contents

Introduction 7

Chapter 1: The Basics Of Cryptocurrency And The Blockchain 9

Chapter 2: Tips For Mining Cryptocurrency 21

Chapter 3: Top 6 Coins You Can Invest In Apart From Bitcoin 29

Chapter 4: Crypto Trading Plan And Building A Diversified Portfolio 36

Chapter 5: Cryptocurrency Trading Foundation 50

Chapter 6: How To Predict Return On Investment And Payback Period Of Cryptocurrencies 63

Chapter 7: Cryptocurrency Fundamental Analysis And Ico Checklist 82

Conclusion 96

Introduction

This book explains everything you need to know about investing in cryptocurrency. Most people ask themselves, why should I invest in cryptocurrency? Which are the best cryptocurrencies to put in my portfolio? How can I store and buy them? Find answers to these and other questions that might be troubling you concerning investing in cryptocurrency.

Crypto or virtual currencies such as Ethereum or Bitcoin are by far the hottest investment inventions currently available. These exchangeable and immutable cryptographic tokens promise to become non-manipulated and hard cash for the entire world. The advocates of crypto see a future where cryptocurrencies like Bitcoin and others coins will substitute Dollar, Euro and so forth and create the first hard and free world currency.

Cryptocurrency is the new trend when it comes to money market, which contains elements of mathematical theory and computer science. Its main function is to protect communications as it convert legible data into unbreakable code. One can track his/her purchases and transfer with cryptocurrency. Whether it is the idea of cryptocurrency or divergence of their portfolio, individuals from different walks of life are investing in digital currencies. If you are somehow new to the concept of crypto and wondering what is going on, here are the basic concepts and considerations for investments in cryptocurrencies.

Chapter 1: The Basics Of Cryptocurrency And The Blockchain

What is Cryptocurrency?

Cryptocurrency is a form of digital currency created using cryptography. Therefore, 'cryptocurrency' is a name derived from the word cryptography, which means being encrypted. In simple, this can be translated directly to mean, a currency that has been verified and encrypted using a digital system. Cryptography technology boomed back in the 1980s when many digital currencies were discovered and availed broadly for use. Investing in this market was such a great risk as most people associated it with robbery, violence and drug addiction, while others thought that it was a pyramid scheme something that exists even today. Currently, investing in Crypto has become a central activity for all. It is very important to understand that cryptocurrency is deeply rooted in the high digital notch. As a result, to access this currency one should be involved in transactions that are carried using digital platforms that use the encrypted software. What the system does is that it controls currency transfer and peer-to-peer transactions without involving any central role players such as the government or the banks. The most interesting thing about the use of cryptocurrency is that it is never affected by inflation or deflation which highly stagnate the extended market using money currency. As a result, most investors opt to invest in crypto coins. An annual record of over 0.5 % increase of new crypto users is a proportional evident to the rampant increase in the mining of the cryptocurrency.

Beginner's Understanding On Cryptocurrency

Cryptocurrency is an ambiguous word for newbies. It is important to note that Cryptocurrency is an anonymous word in the digital market that is trending at an alarming rate. The fact is that trying to understand the whole process is worth everything, bearing in mind that today those with knowledge of digital currency are reaping abnormal profits that nobody can make in the normal money currency market. From records of cryptocurrency statistics, a lot of improvement is taking place with so many beginners flowing in every day.

Well, the future of cryptocurrency is unpredictable with most of its application seeming to be more of a fad. Not until 2017, that cryptocurrency has taken charge of the market with so many members despite the cons and the pros that might affect its future performance. To get an absolute understanding of the digital money, you are required to master the basics of cryptocurrency, majoring on its origin, who founded it, where and when among other facts concerning its history.

History Of Bitcoins And Other Coins

Satoshi Nakamoto discovered Bitcoin mining in the year 2008. This was followed by the publication of white paper writing entitled "A Peer-to-Peer Electronic Cash System." To create a fully decentralized and an independent electronic cash system, Nakamoto relied on two major inventions that he had invented prior to the latter. That is the technology on hash cash and the B-money. Therefore, electronic cash system is a combination of the hash cash and the B-money technology. To understand the system one should first consider establishing a foundation of knowledge about the two types of technologies. Bitcoin mining system is a digital distributed computing technology that is designed to carry out algorithm math after every 10 minutes on a global level. All that matters is that the system network is decentralized to ensure that there is a balanced consensus for the entire transaction and that double spending is avoided ensuring that there is no use of single unit twice.

After the invention of Bitcoin in 2008, the network took a whole year of testing, investigating and verifying. After that, it started operating in 2009. At this time, the entire network sorely depended on Nakamoto's publications and guidelines after which various people started inventing other programs and revising Nakamoto's work. Today, there is a record of rampant increase in Bitcoin resilience and security due to great improvement in the technological advancement of the distributed digital computation system. According to digital currency and financial statistics, the Bitcoins electronic system processing capacity is above any top rated supercomputer in the world today. Currently, the value of Bitcoin in the market is estimated to be $5-$10 billion, which varies depending on the rate at which the dollar and Bitcoin are being exchanged. Bitcoin mining is a decentralized system fully dependent on its computation. This means that it does not involve any central agency or authority to help in making transactions valid, settling payments or issuing of currency among the transacting individuals. The system relies on a proof of work as an indicator that certain transaction took place and that a certain individual upon success earned some brand new Bitcoins. Today, the bitcoin electronic system can instantly process over $150 and release them freely for the peer-peer transaction at a zero cost. No charges are made in such transactions since no middle-man is involved. Additionally, no taxation occurs on this system of transaction.

What Is Bitcoin?

In an ecosystem of digital currency, a combination of technology and concepts under which transactions operate is what is referred as Bitcoin. It is a measured unit of currency that is used to transmit and store a value from one peer to another during transactions, hence forming Bitcoin networks. Internet is the major network through which the bitcoin networking takes place. There are other networking methods for the partners to keep transacting regardless of locations and distance. The whole Bitcoin networking can be stack on software which is easily installed in the computer of Bitcoin user. The software can as well be installed in mobile smartphones, laptops, and the desktops in order to make the market affordable and available to all. Just like the money or any other currency used worldwide, Bitcoin currency can be used by the merchants and the ordinary people as a unit of value for sales and purchases, for crediting and debiting as well as for sending to people among others. The greatest advantage of using Bitcoin currency over money currency is that, they are universal hence can never be limited by borders. Moreover, with bitcoin currency, high security is enhanced since the system is encrypted and endowed with digital features such as digital signing. Most surprisingly, the system is faster, transmitting Bitcoins than any other currency.

Bitcoin Transactions

A Bitcoin transaction is the transfer of value between wallets of Bitcoin in a shared public ledger (blockchain). The entire Bitcoin network relies on the blockchain and everyone on the network has a copy of the blockchain. Bitcoin wallets keep seeds or private keys, which are a secret piece of data. These private keys are used to sign transaction where they provide mathematical evidence that they originate from the owners wallet. These signatures provide security by preventing the transactions alterations by anyone once they are issued. Each transaction is broadcasted between users through a process known as mining. For someone to receive a Bitcoin, you should provide the sender with the generated Bitcoin address. The sender sends a new transaction with their named address as the sender and receiver address as the recipient.

Working of Blockchains

A Bitcoin fundamentally is a very simple data ledger file known as blockchain. This is comparatively small, just like a long text message on a smartphone. A Bitcoin blockchain is made up of three parts: identifying address, history and the private key header log. The identifying address is made up of approximately 34 characters; the history part is the ledger showing who has bought and sold it. The third part is the complex part where a complicated digital signature is captured to confirm every transaction for a particular Bitcoin file.

All devices involved in Bitcoin network maintains and stores a copy of the blockchain. After the users have spent their Bitcoins, the transactions are broadcasted to the network. The new transaction is collected, verified and saved in the blockchain. These latest updates are grouped as data chunks known as blocks. These new blocks are broadcasted to the rest of the network for updates.

All blocks in the blockchain are stored in chronological order. Only new blocks can be added to the blockchain. The already existing blocks cannot be removed or modified. This is done using cryptographic hashing. All new entry blocks must have a hash value to prove that new block exists just after the prior block. Any tamper or modification will unpredictably manipulate the referencing hash value of all the blocks that will follow. This technique maintains the chronology of the blockchain and prevents modification or tampering with existing blocks. Synchronization of transaction and barring of dishonest users is done using public key cryptography and the concept of proof-of-work.

Can Bitcoin Be Created Out Of Thin Air?

Every Bitcoin exists as an entry in the blockchain ledger. These entries describe transactions from sender to recipient. All senders must first be recipients of an existing transaction. For you to be a sender, you must first be a receiver, and this is confirmed or verified using the digital signature. Note that existence and ownership of Bitcoin is only because of a transaction. However, the sole exception to the sender to recipient rule is the transaction that describes newly made Bitcoin (mining). In these transactions, there are no senders only recipients exist. Note that Bitcoins cannot be counterfeited as they can be traced up to their origin.

Aggregation Of Transactions Into Blocks

Once the transaction has been validated, Bitcoin node adds it to the transaction pool, or memory pool, a place where transactions wait until they are mined/included into the block. (A person, for example, Isaac can mine

Bitcoin through 'mining rig' a specifically designed computer hardware system for mining Bitcoin. This dedicated mining hardware is connected to a server that runs a full bitcoin node, which in this case we can call it Isaac node. Although you can as well mine without a full node.) Isaac's node proceeds by collecting, validating and relaying new transactions like other nodes. However, unlike other nodes, Isaac's node will proceed by aggregating this transaction into a candidate block.

A girl by the name Ann wanted some Bitcoins, so she exchanged some cash for it. The transaction was created by Martin, which funded Ann's wallet with about 0.20 BTC. Ann used her bitcoin to buy a mug of tea at Jane's restaurant. Let's now have a look at the blocks that are created when Ann bought a mug of tea from Jane's coffee. Ann's transaction will then be included in block **X** (299,516). Now let's assume that this block is mined by Isaac's mining systems and keenly follow Ann's transaction as it turns out to be part of the new block.

Isaac's mining node will maintain a local copy of blockchain, which will entail a long list of every block that has ever been created since 2009, the beginning of bitcoin system. When Ann purchases a mug of tea, Isaac's node assembles a chain up to block **Z** (299,514). Isaac's node is very keen to listen for every transaction, to try and mine a new block as well as listen to other blocks that are discovered by other nodes. As Isaac's node is busy mining, it gets block **Y** (299,515) through the network of bitcoin. The arrival of this new block implies the end of a very tough competition for block **Y** (299,515) and the start of a new competition to create block **X** (299,516).

For the last ten minutes when the node from Isaac was busy hunting for a solution concerning block **Y** (299,515), it was also busy collecting other several transactions to prepare for the next block. Therefore, at the end of the ten minutes, it will have collected a number of transactions in its memory pool. When it has received block **Y** (277,315) and validated it, Isaac's node will check any transaction in the memory pool and delete all that was contained in block **Y** (299,515). Any transaction that remains the memory pool and is not confirmed remain to be recorded in another block.

Isaac's node instantly constructs another empty block, block 299,316 candidates. The new block is known as candidate block since it's an invalid block since it doesn't contain authentic proof of work. The only way to make a block valid is if a miner successfully finds a solution to the algorithm of proof-of-work.

Chapter 2: Tips For Mining Cryptocurrency

When it comes to mining, many find it hard to comprehend the few steps some of which I have clearly and deeply highlighted in this book. With the vast information out there, you can find extra ideas to make your mining process more effective and productive. In this chapter, I will be glad to share with you some of the tricks and tip that you can apply to ease your crypto mining process.

Tips

A Mining Rig Will Be The First Order Of The Business

As far as the process goes, the mining rig is one of the most competitive you will ever see. Most people in this world find it easy and worth to invest in the mining process, numbers of miners coming up with the latest mining software increase every day. With this in mind, you will want to start with due diligence if you hope to have opportunities in this lucrative field.

Cryptocurrency calculator is a device that can help you with research part. All you got do is enter your important information into the coins miner you are planning on obtaining and see how long you will need to make a profit. To be sincere with you, if you do not have at least a couple hundred of dollars to spend you probably will not make it to any big payoffs.

Once you have completed all your necessary calculations, you can then select your miner. If you are not sure which is the best option for you, you can visit mining websites that have reviewed the best option for you. The newest and most powerful option today is the Antminer S9.

Those interested in this should know that things have changed since the early days of crypto mining when it was possible to perform this action from your computer with a graphics card. This was called GPU mining and is no longer an option; today you will need an ASIC miner, which is a specially built computer to handle this task.

Get A Coin Wallet

Different digital currency may have specific wallet designed for them. Before you even go further, you will need to get a good wallet and ensure the passwords are secure. You will need a place to hold your valuable coins. The wallet is now very easy to get but important to manage properly. Once you have your cryptocurrency wallet you will need to obtain the address. The process has been explained in detail in part of this book.

In case you decide to use a self-hosted wallet, which is a program downloaded onto your computer as opposed to an online service, you will have another crucial step to make. What you will need is a copy of your wallet .dat file stored somewhere safe like on a thumb drive. The reason you will need this is in the event your computer crashes. Without a copy of your wallet.dat file, you could lose all your collected coins. They will not go to another person, they just vanish like burning paper money.

Get A Good Mining Pool

Find yourself a good mining pool, there are many advantages when you join a pool. A mining pool is like a group of crypto miners that combine their collected computation power to produce even more coins at a go. In the mining pool, you will be given an easier algorithm to work on and the combination of efforts will make it quite possible to solve the larger algorithms and earn the block of cryptocurrency that will be divided among the team of miners. This makes the advent of obtaining the coins block a more frequent. You will be making your personal ROIS much faster because you will be working in combination with other miners.

Properly Selecting Your Mining Pool Will Require Asking Some Important Questions:

- What is the reward method? You will want to know if rewards are proportional, PPLNS or score based

- What is the mining fee and charge withdrawing funds?

- How frequently are blocks uncovered?

- How easy is the withdrawal process?

- What kind of stats does this pool provide?

- How stable is this pool?

Have A Computer-mining Program

Having the basics, you can begin mining, but you will need a mining client that will handle the operations of your rig from your personal computer. This will help in effective monitoring of your rig. The software you chose will be specific to the mining rig you selected. Many of this mining rig has their own mining software be careful when installing one.

Organize A VPS

Having a VPS will make the whole process of mining coins a lot easier and more secure. A VPS will allow a far greater degree of privacy when using digital currency, and quality offerings such as liberty VPS are better, secure and can run anonymously.

Tricks

Choose The Right GPU

There are mainly just two GPUs - AMD and NVidia. Go for AMD. Now while choosing AMD, you will see same modes coming straight from Sapphire and from others like XFX Gigabyte MSI. Always try to go for Sapphire originals and never go for MSI.

Drivers

For 280-290, cards go with 15.12 drivers. For new cards, go with the newest driver and their new feature called Radeon Chill.

System

While I know most people love Linux. Windows is king for mining. That is because the best miners are made and updated the fastest on windows. Running them is also very easy - mostly click and play. Currently, Claymore makes best miners, and there was no ZEC Linux version of this at all. Go for Windows.

Make Rig At Least 5 Gpus

You spent money on parts, and now you want to mine with 3-4 cards? Doesn't make any sense. Add at least one or two cards.

Windows 7 it will see just 4 cards. Here is a driver that lets you have as many cards as you wish for the system. DOWNLOAD

Windows 10 sees all GPUs right away but uses a little more of resources, so it is better to run Window 7.

Use USB Risers

Risers are things connecting your computer with the GPU. Currently, technology went ahead, and it is better to use USB ones. They are more efficient and stable.

Cool Down Old GPUs

This trick is brilliant. If used properly will keep your cards alive forever!

Once a year unscrew four screws from GPU, clean this rectangle of old paste and put new thermal paste on it.

Above you can see my AMD 280x and the old paste on it.

Edit Virtual Memory

Windows had odd virtual memory, and while running few cards on your rig, you have to edit it to 16 GB.

Just go to: Computer Properties -> Advanced System Settings -> Performance -> Advanced -> Virtual Memory

Chapter 3: Top 6 Coins You Can Invest In Apart From Bitcoin

Investing in cryptocurrencies is an arms race which rewards quick adopters. Bitcoin has not only been a trendsetter, ushering in the wave of cryptocurrency that is built on a decentralized network of peer-to-peer, it has become de facto standard in the cryptocurrency industry. Other currencies which are inspired by Bitcoin are collectively known as Altcoins and have really tried to present themselves as improved or modified version of Bitcoin. Even though most of these currencies are simple and easier to invest-in compared to Bitcoin, there are several tradeoffs like bigger risk brought on by lesser retention, value, and acceptance. In this book we will focus mainly on six main altcoins, selected from over 700, though not in any specific order.

Ethereum (ETH)

It was launched in 2015 and is a decentralized software platform which allows Distributed Applications

(ÐApps) and Smart Contracts to be built and run without any interference, fraud, downtime or control from a third party. In 2014, Ethereum launched a pre-sale for ether which actually received an overwhelming response. Ether, a platform-specific cryptographic token is the applications that Ethereum are run on. Therefore, we can be able to say that ether is like a vehicle that moves around on Ethereum platform, which is sought by different developers who are looking to run and develop applications inside Ethereum. As a matter of fact, according to Ethereum, it can as well be used to "decentralize, codify, trade and secure about anything." Due to the attack in 2006 on the DAO, Ethereum split into Ethereum Classic (ETC) and Ethereum (ETH). The market capitalization of Ethereum (ETH) is $4.4 billion, which is second after Bitcoin among other cryptocurrencies.

The biggest project Ethereum (ETH) has seen of late is the partnership between Microsoft with ConsenSys that offers EBaaS (Ethereum Blockchain as a Service) on Microsoft Azure in that Enterprise developers and clients can have a single click cloud-based blockchain developer environment. In 2017, ETH made a very big move when it established the Enterprise Ethereum Alliance that focused on promoting and building the best standards and practices to effectively facilitate the adoption of Ethereum procedure for the enterprise. Some of the greatest brands from insurance, consultancy, technology, and banking are part of Enterprise Ethereum.

Litecoin (LTC)

Launched in 2011, Litecoin was among the first cryptocurrencies following Bitcoin and was mostly referred by most people as "silver to Bitcoins gold." Charlie Lee who was a former Google engineer and MIT graduate created it. Litecoin is majorly built on an open source world payment network which isn't controlled by any authority and uses "scrypt" like a proof of work that could be recorded with the assistance of CPUs of customer grade. Therefore, making it a well decentralized open source. As it can be seen, Litecoin was built with an objective of improving the shortcomings of Bitcoins and over the years it has earned the support of the industry along with high liquidity and trade volume. It have a quicker block generation rate, thereby offering faster transaction confirmation. Apart from developers, there is a high growing number of merchants who accept it.

Litecoin is created to be able to produce more coins, about four times than Bitcoin, and at a faster rate of about a quarter of Bitcoin's time. Generally, Litecoin has been seen as 2nd to Bitcoins in terms of value, although Litecoins are more easily transactional and obtainable.

Zcash (ZEC)

Zcash is an open-source and decentralized cryptocurrency, which was launched in latter part of 2016, and it looks very promising. For example, if *HTTP* in Bitcoin is for money, then *https* is Zcash: this is how Zcash defines themselves. It offers selective transparency and privacy of transactions. Just like *https*, Zcash has seen to claim that they provide extra privacy or security where every transaction is published and recorded on the blockchain, but other details like amount, recipient, and sender remain private. The users of Zcash are offered a choice of 'shielded transactions' that allow all content to be encrypted through the use of the advanced cryptographic method or a zk-SNARK a zero-knowledge proof contraction developed by the team of Zcash.

In other words of Zcash is a new cryptocurrency and blockchain that allows private transactions or generally private information in a public blockchain. It allows new apps, consumer, and businesses to control who should see the details of one's transactions, even when they are using a global, un-permission blockchain.

Monero (XMR)

This is said to be an untraceable, private and secure currency. Monero is an open-source cryptocurrency, which was launched in 2014 and it spiked impressive interest among the cryptography enthusiasts and community. Development of Monero cryptocurrency is totally community-driven and donation-based. This cryptocurrency was launched with a strong emphasis on scalability and decentralization, and it allows complete privacy through the usage of a special technique known as "ring signatures." Availability of this technique, it looks like a group of cryptographic signatures that includes at least one actual participant, however since all of them appear valid, the real one can't be isolated.

Individuals transacting in Monero could change it back to dollars or to either Bitcoin via a number of online cryptocurrency exchanges. If the usage of Monero is perceived to be of questionable activity or illegal, then its widespread use can be dampened.

Ripple (XRP)

This is a real-time global settlement network which offers low-cost, certain and instant international payments. Ripple (XRP) "enables commercial banks to settle their cross-border payments faster and in real time, at lower costs, and with end-to-end transparency." Ripple currency was released in 2012, and it has $1.26 billion market capitalization. The consensus ledger of Ripple -- its conformation method – does not need mining, thereby reducing network latency and minimizes the use of computing power. Ripple mainly believes that 'distribution value is a powerful method to incentivize specific behaviors'. Hence it is currently planning to distribute XRP mainly "through enterprise development deals, incentives to liquidity providers who propose tighter spreads for payments, as well as selling XRP to institutional buyers interested in investing in XRP."

Dash

Dash was initially known as Darkcoin, it's Bitcoin's more secretive version. It offers more anonymity as it works on a network which is decentralized, hence making their transactions almost untraceable. Dash was launched in January 2014, it experienced an escalating fan following in a small span of time. Evan Duffield was the one who created this cryptocurrency, and it can be mined using a GPU or CPU. At around March 2015, Dash was rebranded from Darkcoin, which stands for Digital Cash and works under the ticker – DASH. Even after rebranding, they did not change any of their technological features like InstantX, Darksend, etc.

Chapter 4: Crypto Trading Plan And Building A Diversified Portfolio

With the increasing number of investors in the field of cryptocurrency, there is need to have knowledge and content about it. Knowing how to plan for a trade and having a diversified crypto portfolio gives a trader a greater edge to thrust in the market. This chapter will educate you the reason why you should have a good cryptocurrency portfolio, a trading plan and the discipline to follow to the latter.

Crypto Trading Plan

A trading plan is a roadmap that has a set of guidelines that clearly define trading objectives and outline various way of achieving the set objectives. It helps one to focus on executing the strategies. There are two broad types of traders in cryptocurrency, the discretionary and system traders. The discretionary traders are traders who monitor the market and place manual trade in accordance with the information that is available while the system traders utilize a level of trade automation to implement rules.

Stock Markets

When planning to trade in cryptocurrency, make a consideration on the stock markets that you will trade on. Among the trading markets are bonds, commodities, Exchange trade funds, Forex, future, options and popular e-mini futures contract. The choice of instrument of use must be of good liquidity and validity to maximize chances of gaining profit.

Liquidity is the ease to sell and buy shares. Markets that will trade with tight bids and with enough market depth to fill orders as soon as possible have good liquidity. It ensures orders will be field with minimal spillage and without affecting the prices.

On the other hand, validity measures the speed at which prices move up and down in a particular market, when a trading commodity becomes volatile, the traders get an opportunity to profit from the changes in prices weather the variation was a rise or a fall.

Chart Interval To Use In Making Trading Decisions

Chart intervals are associated with a trading style basing them on volumes, or activities. Long-term traders prefer longer period charts in their trading and short-term traders use short-term trading charts. A short chart interval can last for 60 minutes while a long-term chart can last for more than that. For example, a scalper may prefer a 144-tick chart to a swing trader, who would use the 60 minutes chart,

A defined trading plan must show indicators that apply to the chart even though indicators alone provide signals for buying and selling. A trader should interpret the signals to find entry and exit points that are suitable for his trading style.

Position Sizing

A position size is the dollar value of a cryptocurrency that one is trading in. The trader account size and risk tolerance should be taken in to account to determining an appropriate sizing. Position sizing is the size of a position with a particular portfolio. A trader may decide to start with one future contract. After the system becomes successful, the trader can decide to invest in other contracts. Trading in more than one contract increases the chances of high profit margins as it minimizes chances of loses. Regardless of the positioning size of investors, all rules are stated in the trading plan.

Entry In The Trade With Filters And Triggers

People are different in the way they make an entry in trade. Consistent method while making an entry is having already set trading rules in place. Some traders will take their time, monitor from the sideline still waiting to make an entry and invest. This most of the time leaves them at the verge of missing big trading opportunities. They are conservative traders while the aggressive traders may grab any opportunity that is available to invest. Trade rules accommodate both this two characters and they can benefit using trade triggers and filters. Trade filters includes a variety of factors ranging from time of day to location of price. For example, a price bar in a chat may close in a set of time when using a moving average, this triggers the opening of another entry with a stop order set above the previous bar

Exit Rules

An entry in the cryptocurrency at any level can yield a profit when you decide to exit at the opportune time. Exit points are critical because they define the success of the trade. Some of the trade outcomes when exiting include: profit levels, stop and reverse strategies and time exits such as end of day.

Building Diversified Crypto Portfolio

A good structure of a cryptocurrency portfolio gives you a long-term exposure to a diversified group of coins. It also plays a higher risk-reward game in the median and short-term. People who are making much profit in cryptocurrency for example bitcoin are not only buying the coins, they are leveraging the bitcoin with altcoins such as ether largely, Monero and litecoins to make more money. The main frameworks that one can use are:

1. Function: look if the products are defendable and have a functional niche.
2. Size of community/adoption: check the frequency in which investors use the coin.
3. Technology: you need to know if the framework technology solves problem with novel methods.
4. Aligned incentives and governance: the investors need to be systematically aligned to the incentives.
5. Market opportunity: the size of the market and the market cap should be understood.

Core Assets

This are the major currencies, every cryptocurrency investor should start with a bitcoin and Ether. Bitcoins are the highly traded of all coins in the market. They have proven to be the currency that stores value and have a fast mover advantage compared to altcoins. Ethereum gives room for greater innovations that are to come over the next ten years through blockchain technology. It has a bigger chance of storing value. Ether shows great potential for future as a cryptocurrency and both as a blockchain. A bitcoin mostly continues to grow as anticipated before it forks. The coin gains volatility highly.

Platform Cryptocurrency

These set of coins resolve problems through the blockchain technology.

A ripple coin for example works on the international payment remittance market while NEO will provide a platform to extend contracts. A ripple is a blockchain enablement for money transfer. Its volatility for growth can get as high as 10 times. A ripple provides a blockchain enabled competing System to swift for sending payments.

A litecoin is a kind of buffer to a bitcoin and can grow together. A litecoin has the opportunity of up to 7% volatility. This coin has the potential to rise after a long bitcoin has shoot. This technology is cheap to acquire thus people consider it as an alternative when they want to diversify coins at the fourth or fifth coin petition

Small Coins

Monero similar to a bitcoin since it allows value exchange. They differ in the aspect that a difference is that a monero coin provides greater privacy to those that utilize their blockchains using the stitch address mechanism.

Zcash is a decentralized and open source cryptocurrency launched in the late 2016. It offers privacy and transparency in trade. It offers its users the option of shield transaction that allows for content encryption.

The figure below shows the market cap (value of token) for top coins in trade.

How To Build A Crypto Portfolio

Step 1: Open A Cryptocurrency Account

Opening an account with a cryptocurrency exchange is the first step to buying cryptocurrencies. Choose a name for your portfolio then choose a currency that you want to trade in. If you want to trade in bitcoin, you can buy the coins from your fiat money. To do this you have to make sure the exchange platform you pick accept fiat deposits such as dollars and Euros. Altcoins exist on specific cryptoexchange platforms. Examples of recommended crypto exchange include FX open and

FX choice. You can also buy coins from brokers that trade in bitcoins and altcoins. The best brokers include coinbase and poloniex among others.

Step 2: Select Long-term Investment Coins

There are many cryptocurrencies available in the exchange platforms across the world ranging from bitcoins, ethereum, ripple, and litecoins among other altcoins. To get the right coin you need to look at the market cap, the price variation, the volumes, circulating supplies and the changes that have occurred in the charts of a particular coin. Through this evaluation, you are able to know which cons are worth investing in the long term. It is wise to keep in mind that there are large caps (these are the top five coins), mid caps and small caps which are smaller than 200 million dollars. Investing in large and mid caps is likely to yield good results.

Step 3: Know The Price Of Your Preferred Cryptocurrency

For a trader to flourish in the cryptocurrencies trade they should know the price at which the cryptocurrency is trading at. This maximizes chances of profit making and market dominating. A trader should always apply the buy low and sell high principle if they want to gain in the trade.

Step 4: Have A Cryptocurrency Wallet

All the bitcoin and altcoins should be stored in a cryptocurrency wallet, a bank account for the coins. Each cryptocurrency coin has its own wallet. For example, a bitcoin is stored in a bitcoin wallet, an ethereum is stored in an ethereum wallet. These wallets communicate to specific coin nodes. The blockchain respond when you want to transact. The cryptocurrency can be stored online or offline.

How Do You Build A Cryptocurrency Portfolio With 500 Dollars?

Many cryptocurrencies exist in the market, this makes it difficult to predict which one will rise in price and which one will stagnate. Firstly, check for coins that have a real life value and a strong development potential. Invest in coins that are not pre-mined. When you have 500 dollars and hope to build a cryptocurrency portfolio, the following are the coins that will best utilize this amount to yield the desired profit.

Ethereum: It is the mother of all coin and the most important one to invest. It has a growth rate of over 3500% and firmly remains in the second position in the market. It serves as the basis of decentralization app of the ecosystem. In 2016-2017, the value of ether rose from 6 dollars to 1000 dollar. This is evident that a large investment in Ether will increase profit if stocked for a long time. Therefore, I recommend that 200 dollars of the investment portfolio be on ethereum. Ether takes much stock than a bitcoin due to its ability to make more profit margins.

Bitcoin: Digital coins are slowly gaining acceptance as form of payment in the world with bitcoin being the top most coins in the trade. With the diversification of education and increasing knowledge in blockchain technology, a big investment in a bitcoin in your portfolio is recommendable. One year ago a bitcoin that sold for 650 dollars trades at around 16000 today. Therefore 1500 dollars of the portfolio should buy the Bitcoin.

Monero: Most traders in cryptocurrency are shifting to privatization in the Market. It is a community driven and donation-base cryptocurrency that is in place since April 2014. It focuses on decentralization and scalability using ring signatures. It is the leading coin in privatization. 100 dollars of the cryptocurrency portfolio coin should buy this coin.

Litecoin: It has a potential to lead in unveiling solutions for future market development. In May 2017, Litecoin became the first of top five (by market cap) cryptocurrency to adopt segregated witness. The network processes a block in every 2.5 minutes to allow faster deposits. I would recommend 100 dollars of the cryptocurrency investment to buy litecoins.

- Bitcoin – 1500 dollars
- Ether – 1500 dollars
- Litecoin – 100 dollars
- Monera – 100 dollar

It is possible to get a large profit margin when one makes an entry in the cryptocurrency trade with 5000 dollars.

Chapter 5: Cryptocurrency Trading Foundation

Having a good foundation in the cryptocurrency world is an advantage, as one will know which moves will lead to loss or profit generation. A trader needs to have vast knowledge on know the various exchange platforms, the tycoons in the field and learn from their experiences. Through this, he is able to know the traps to avoid and the best way to trade.

The Different Types Of Traders
There are different types of investors in cryptocurrency, one of them hold the coins hoping to sell when it is worth millions. Others spend their coins for their daily needs while others exchange coins frequently looking for quick cash.

The Holder Trader
This enthusiast invests in bitcoins and altcoins for long-term purposes. No matter how volatile the market

is, these traders cannot sell their coins. They do not care about a fall in price until something extraordinary happens in the market cap. The advantage of this trader is that they can yield a lot of money when they exit. They also risk losing very thing.

The Spender Trader

These traders believe cryptocurrency coins are for spreading and spend. They believe spending the digital assets with Merchants, business and giving the currencies to new comers helps the economy. There are companies that pay their employees and other bills using the bitcoins.

New Comers

Many people are venturing in cryptocurrency, a number of them do not know what they are doing. These traders have many questions as they seek to gain content in the trade. Some lose their assets before they know how the market works. When they get help instances of swindle and fraud reduce.

The Maximist

This person believes that the bitcoin is the only cryptocurrency that matters. They believe that the altcoins have no real value. Most of these traders cannot consider any discussion about the altcoins.

Top Three Crypto Traders

Many types of traders ventured in to cryptocurrency over the last few years. This is due to the potential of making big money. The following are the top traders in bitcoin without regards to the current ranking in market cap.

Whale Panda

Whale panda has done thorough research on cryptocurrency. He tracks side projects and niche innovations before they hit more mainstream radar, the trader delivers insights and tips on the platform with wit and humor. Whale panda trades in bitcoins and several altcoins. He has platform on twitter shows how he is influential in cryptocurrency trade as other persons interested.

Cryptoyoda

Cryptoyoda is a cryptocurrency Investor and a technical analyst who is passionate about his work. He currently has over 50,000 followers and for good reason. He posts materials about cryptocurrency world and the latest information of the same.

The Digital Currency Advisor

He is a former Wall St. Hedge Fund Manager is a veteran in the trade. He is a professional trader in both retail and institutions at Altcoins Advisory. His passion lies in venturing in the blockchain technology. At the top notch in Macro trading, Swing trading, finding undervalued cryptocurrencies, and predicting price movements.

Trading Psychology

In order to be a successful trader and yield more profit than loses in cryptocurrency trade one requires various skills and characteristics that are unique to the trade. One must be aware of the fundamentals of the trading company and be able to identify trends that mark the key traits needed.

Sometimes a trader's stock fluctuates on short notices. For this reason he has to make decisions to keep the trade going. He also needs to be disciplined so that they stick to their business plan. A focused trader will learn to master trading traps to prevent loses that could otherwise be avoided. A trader needs to get over the following:

Greed

When a trader becomes greedy, he will always want more of what he is getting. He rarely realizes the risk that awaits him with all the value that he has added and the profit that he has generated; greedy traders do not know when to stop. This is their downfall because they end up losing everything they have gained as assets, returns and profit. It is difficult to get over greed since every trader wants to trade big and make the business better. For example if a bitcoin value when you bought was worth $10, then the trader can sell it when it is at $15. A trader should ensure that his mindset is clear, and maintain a level of rational business decision as in his business plan.

Fear

Fear is a natural reaction to a threat in business. Understanding one's fear should be the head start of any trader in cryptocurrency. It is common for fear to encroach you if there are pulsating sigs of stock reduction, when your coins have decreased in value according to the market, a trader who understands the implication of fear will not allow the situation to compel him to liquidate the assets and crash because they could not take risk. When you do not take risks, you will miss on the gains. Having alternative plans when making a business plan saves many traders the stress. For instance, one can buy many altcoins for stocking.

When fear and greed takes over a trader is at risk of loss at any time. Traders should create their trading rules before the start of business. This helps to keep their head in the right place before they feel. Establishing limits while laying out guidelines based on the risk reward relationship for when they will exit a trade.

Traders in cryptocurrency should also consider setting limits on the amount they win or lose in a day. If they reap on $x profit, they are done for the day, if they lose $y then that is the close of business. This is a good strategy because it saves one the risk of losing more.

After a period of trade, a trader should periodically review their performance including the losses and gains, individual positions, the business progress in terms of knowledge gained among other things. It is always an opportunity to retrace where mistakes were made and to cover loopholes. It helps them to maintain the right psychology to run the trade and flourish in the market.

Best Cryptocurrency Trading Exchange

Binance

Binance has existed since 2017 and has gained popularity since then. It has become a first mover exchange for listing new altcoins earlier that just about anyone else in the industry. Unlike with some other exchanges, when one is dealing with Binance they have the opportunity to interface with two different trading UIs. Once you get the drop of these interfaces though, the advanced set-up has many great benefits. It allows you to conduct historical and projective technical analyses on given crypto coins at your leisure. New users who have not passed the first level have a withdrawal limit. However, if they achieve level 2 verification, then they will be allowed to withdrawal as many as 100 bitcoins each and every day. It is worth it to verify if you are doing massive trades.

KuCoin

It is a trade exchange company based out of South Korea. It has one of the easiest UIs to use. KuCoin confirms your crypto deposits in a short time span giving traders time to trade right away. One KuCoin Shares (KCS) ERC-20 token is a proprietary aspect of the trade exchange that gives users a great discount on platform fees for making trades in KuCoin Shares instead of, bitcoin or ether. KCS token returns 90 percent of the exchange fee to the user. Users get dividend of the ether just for holding KCS. It has a strong customer support that they avail.

GDAX

It is one of the most popular cryptocurrency exchange-trading outlets in America. It provides fewer trading pairs than other popular exchange. It gives opportunity to trade between Bitcoin, Ethereum, Litecoin and fiat currencies like USD and Euro. It capitalizes on stock as you can get any amount you need. It recently launched its support for bitcoin cash. When using coinbase exchange one can use credit cards or link a bank account if they are buying in bulk. It has advantage over other platforms because it is more secure.

Gemini

It is a United States Based cryptocurrency exchange that only allows investors to become Members and trade in the interface. It was founded by the Tech Venture Capital Twins in 2015. To become a member, you send them an email address. They respond by sending a registration token that a buyer has to redeem back on the Gemini site. After configuration, the exchange process then starts. It has a wide access because it has no deposit and withdrawal fees. One only pays a 0.25 % trading fee.

Bittrex

It is a type of trading exchange that that has over 300 trading pairs based in U.S. Its most popular trading pairs are BTC and ETH. Currently Bittrex does not offer any fiat-to-crypto pairs, e.g. with U.S. dollars, Euros, or British pounds.

Top Seven Habit Of A Successful Trader

1. Be A Risk Taker

On its most fundamental level, cryptocurrency trade is a risk. There is no guarantee of possible win. Good traders understand and accept a certain amount of risk when cutting deals. Understanding risk can save one emotional torment in hard times. It makes it easy to see a loss in failure.

2. Be A Vast Researcher

People lose huge assets in the cryptocurrency trade because of being green in the market. The market can be unpredictable when one enters without knowledge of exchange platforms, available technology and best currencies to invest in among other factors. Thorough research is mandatory for one to be a successful trader in this field. Keep journals of trade, analyze both published and unpublished work to enrich yourself about the trade before making an investment.

3. Be Disciplined And Keep Record

Being discipline in terms of following your trade plans and investment strategies makes you a better trader in cryptocurrency. Discipline gives you the self-drive to know how to utilize assets such that you will not run out of stock. Keep records of coins sold, stock exchanged and stoke bought. Use screenshots to illustrate just how the trade looked before you placed your orders. Successful traders will use their records to analyze their performance.

4. Have A Passion For Trading The Markets

If you do not have love for the cryptocurrency trade then you will give up along the way before you become successful. Most successful traders are fueled by their passion to keep going even when the risks are more and they feel discouraged.

5. Be Patient

Patience is a virtue that is present in just but a few human beings. It enables a trader to know the best time to make an exit or to make an entry. If he leaves too early, he will not maximize his profit margin. A good trader exercises patients throughout the trade.

6. Stick To Your Routines

Cryptocurrency trading is a process driven activity, for one to realize big profit margins, you must flawlessly execute your trading edge in the markets everyday spend time monitoring how the stock market changes and be consistency in the processes, through this you will be at par with any changes in the market gap.

7. Have The Ability To Adapt To Different Markets

A good trader has the ability to recognize the market and know when it is low or at its peak. A good trade profits from the market conditions when he is aggressive. The trader can opt to stock and not trade their capital waiting for the market to stabilize.

Chapter 6: How To Predict Return On Investment And Payback Period Of Cryptocurrencies

Investing In Cryptocurrencies

At the beginning of April 2016, the total cryptocurrency capital market was estimated to be around $8 billion. Currently, it is just over $12 billion. This shows an over 50% increment, nevertheless, this can be misleading. An understanding of the crypto-coin content and expertise in the investment field is required to obtain optimal exposure into blockchain technology investment. The technologies pushing these cryptocurrency works requires more than just transactions. In future, we will witness all-around better solutions. For a prudent investor, the vital thing is to determine the cryptocurrency that will cater for the true need and not just a fad of a short period.

In the investing world, we have several general rules to follow. However, some are more important than the others are. One of the key things to consider is the longevity, not just of the product, but also the producer of the product. For how long will the service be relevant? How is the ease of the competitors to out-perform this cryptocurrency? Are the developers committed?

Therefore, the key issues we are looking here are

1. A growing and current demand for it.
2. No evidence of imminent competing threats.
3. A team of developers who are committed.

With all this on the cause, then there is a potentially good risk to rewards.

Another big thing to consider is always seeking platform and not features. Most cryptocurrencies are feature works. That explains why only around 30 of cryptocurrencies are viable today. The other 720 plus are useless long-term investments. Coins like Bitcoins and Ethereum have enormous momentum, backing, and multi-cryptocurrency wallet and are examples of platform-based work. They are easy to be operated by the masses and avails a real-life use case.

A Statistical Analysis Of Cryptocurrency

Understanding the risks involved in any investment is very vital. This is done by analyzing statistical properties of this cryptocurrencies as determined by market capitalization. Their exchange rate is versus the US dollar. Returns are non-normal; nevertheless, no distribution fits well jointly to all blockchain technology analyzed. For the commonly used currency like Litecoin and Bitcoin, the generalized hyperbolic distribution gives the best line of fit. For the smaller blockchain technology the generalized t distribution, Gaussian distribution, and Laplace distribution give the best fits. The results are important for risk management purpose and investment.

Bitcoin, as the first decentralized blockchain technology, has benefited greatly from the financial industry, academics, and the media. It has set itself as the leader of the cryptocurrency and is not going to slow any near soon. Growing need for Bitcoin has skyrocketed in the recent months like for example the UK federal government is considering paying out research grants in Bitcoins. So many IT companies are stockpiling on Bitcoin to shield against ransomware.

Chairperson of the board of governors of the US Federal Reserve has encouraged central bankers to study the new innovations in the industry.

Many cryptocurrencies have emerged. However Bitcoin remains the most popular with cryptocurrency market representation of 81%. The main six cryptocurrencies, which have stayed for over two years and covered 90% of the market, include Bitcoin, Litecoin, Ripple, Monero, Dogecoin, and Dash. The data used in this statistical analysis are the historical global indices of cryptocurrency for a period of over two years. Most cryptocurrency exhibit heavy tails. The results obtained after the analysis indicate that none of the distributions that were used gives the best fit jointly for all cryptocurrency.

Litecoin and Bitcoin had the best line of fit using generalized hyperbolic distribution. Ripple, Dash, and Monero had the best fit using the normal inverse Gaussian distribution. Dogecoin had the best line of fit using t distribution. The outcome of this results are in areas of risk management and also for the purpose of investment.

Ideal Investment Strategies

Ethereum and Bitcoin are highly disruptive cryptocurrencies by looking at the advantages of blockchain technologies that drive technology in numerous industries. To come out with an ideal investment strategy, we analyze the historical performance and the extrapolated performance of this cryptocurrencies. Working with the industry professionals has helped to identify the most impactful and probable factors for the future demand of cryptocurrency. Cryptocurrencies speculative nature and volatility create a need for diversification across platforms.

Fiat currency comes into existence because it was able to be controlled and regulated by governments. Nevertheless, it comes with a set of issues. As a way to fix these issues, there was emergent of cryptocurrency around the year 2009. This is a leveraged disruptive technology called blockchain.

In the recent times, the popularity of cryptocurrency has increased. This has prompt investors to determine how to invest into this asset. As a new technology to invest in it, there are many factors to consider to predict their future. To make an informed decision, it is important to check the potential applications, network difficulties and other foreseeable limitations in future as well as origin of the technology. We aim to predict the price of Bitcoin and Ethereum in the next five years through a qualitative and quantitative analysis. From this prediction, we will be able to make appropriate investments.

Bitcoin is the most used and widely known cryptocurrency in the world. It has a current capitalization market of over $10 billion (cryptocurrency market capitalization 2016). The original aim of creating Bitcoin currency was to eliminate trusted third party financial institutions. Bitcoin achieves this by, increasing efficiency, eliminating the possibility of fraud and providing security and validity of a transaction. Bitcoins work by increasing efficiency and reducing unnecessary costs and time of using several financial institutions to equip transactions. Bitcoin is very adaptable in the markets which lack customary financial infrastructure but do have access to mobile data and markets with high and inflated currency which require equipment to allow for the exchange of currency and mobilization.

Ethereum, on the other hand, has the advantage of the application of Smart Contracts within its code. The total market capitalization of Ethereum is approximately 10% that of Bitcoin. The appreciation and depreciation value of Ethereum lies in its ability to eliminate financial institutions in future.

Bitcoin and Ethereum are both mined by solving complex computational problems. Both have additional difficulties in mining as more blocks are added into the blockchain.

Using historical data to predict values for cryptocurrencies is very difficult since there are no sufficient data to extrapolate future prices without a doubt. By examining the trend of the price of Bitcoin in five years is $2250 representing a growth of 301 percent. Ethereum has an extrapolated five-year value of approximately $ 88 that represents growth of 634%. This shows a tremendous growth rate, which is as a result of adoption and hype in the early stage of its life cycle. On deeper analysis, this volatility and high growth of Ethereum and Bitcoin is as a result speculation and hype. This is indicated by the high correlation between Google search and prices of Bitcoins. The time series correlation between Google search and price is 0.64 for Bitcoin and a higher value for Ethereum of 0.88.

For the purpose of accounting for the hype in the regression forecast, the importance of spikes as a result of increased hype and Google searches were discounted by a value of 30 percent. The prices are very much depressed when speculation and hype covering each currency is decreased by a factor of 30 percent. There was a growth rate of approximately 300% for Bitcoin and reduction of 506% for Ethereum on depression impact of Google searches. Even though the reduced importance speculation and hype does lessen this prediction of Ethereum, it has experienced more growth, especially in the recent past.

Speculation-Discounted Price model (bitcoin on left axis, Ethereum on right axis, in USD)

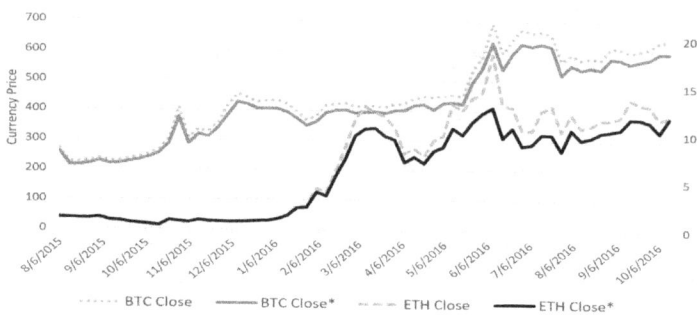

Even though Ethereum looks like a better investment in regard to this analysis, past result do not indicate future performance. Again looking at the high volatility of these currencies, and absence of extensive history this predictions cannot be relied on in the final decision.

In order to have a strong prediction, talks and interviews were arranged with several professionals and experts of cryptocurrency as well as enthusiast traders. Every individual was polled on probability of various occurrences, which affect the demand of every cryptocurrency. They were also required to rate the probable level of impact on the cryptocurrency.

New markets

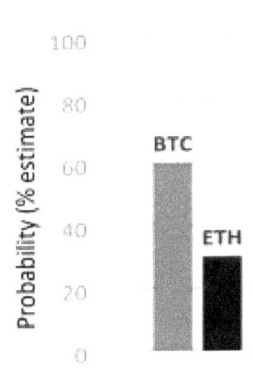

Countries with less developed financial infrastructure but with high smartphone usage are potential markets in which cryptocurrencies can be leveraged. A good example is Kenya where half of its GDP is operated by digital currency. Such countries can take advantage of cryptocurrency in terms of moving money in and out of the country. Bitcoin can offer a great potential for the upcoming markets, as it is widely adopted cryptocurrency. There are over 14 million Bitcoins in circulation with the lowest level of volatility and the highest level of adoption.

Financial Institutions

There has been willingness by the financial institutions to adopt cryptocurrency technology. This is a move to access untapped markets and drive operational efficiencies. But large financial institutions have shown unwillingness to adopt a specific currency. Even though cryptocurrency technology is very likely to be adopted by financial institutions, it is very unlikely that Ethereum or Bitcoin currencies will be widely taken by these organizations.

Regulations And Deregulations

Permissive regulations in the western countries has benefited Bitcoin. Nevertheless, it has experienced restrictions in the western countries. The banning of Bitcoins in China greatly affected its value price. This indicates the importance of global acceptance of cryptocurrency to push up its value.

In order for cryptocurrencies to receive a wide world acceptance, there must be regulations to ensure secure and safe transactions. Deregulation would cause a significant value growth of Bitcoins and ease of transactions across borders. On the other hand Ethereum will not have much value addition, but will experience widespread global adoption.

Major Network Compromise

In such a highly complex network with the anonymous exchange of data, the chances of 'hacks' as an example of network compromise are very high. Ethereum has experienced hacks where a significant amount of ether units has been siphoned. Such a major hack is quite unlikely to happen with Bitcoin because of its rigid framework and relative Lack of widespread utility. More freedom, more nodes and the higher the chances of hacking as in the Ethereum network. Risk of hacks is evident in both Bitcoin and Ethereum trades. However, this is not an indication of flaws in blockchain technology. History has shown that hacks do affect the price of each cryptocurrency.

Global Economic Event

The utility of Bitcoin is strictly digital currency. Due to this, it is expected to have an inverse relationship to the state of world economy. Areas with highly inflated currency or lacking financial infrastructure can use Bitcoin as an alternative means of transaction. Ethereum also has an inverse relation, but with lesser magnitude due to innovative nature of Ethereum network and a wide array of uses. Bitcoin values act like commodities while that of Ethereum relate closely to widespread adoption of the network as well as smart contracts.

E-commerce

Both Ethereum and Bitcoin exhibits potential of their values to be positively impacted by e-commerce. Nevertheless, Bitcoin stands a higher chance to be used for trade. Payment systems are in such a way that they take a long time to be processed. Cryptocurrency reduces this transaction time. Bitcoin offers a better solution for this unlike Ethereum, which has a greater potential for hacks.

Financial Technology

The cryptocurrency applications for financial applications favors more the Ethereum as it is more flexible for the institutions to carry out operations. There is a secure transaction as well as a single ledger that shrinks the need to reconcile across every party independent ledger. Individual currencies could benefit if the financial companies increase liquidity in low liquidity markets, nevertheless, this is quite a small opportunity. Ethereum smart contracts provide a wider range of applications. Financial technology organizations would find it easier to adapt to Ethereum as they can carry out additional applications in addition to leveraging the benefits of Bitcoin as blockchain technology.

Quantitative Analysis

Several assumptions need to be made in order to assist in compiling a quantitative analysis to assist in a five-year prediction for each of the cryptocurrency. A total of 100 simulations (Monte Carlo) are run in order to compile an expected return on each currency after five years. Bitcoin outperformed Ethereum in 58 out of 100 simulations. This was largely because of high variance of outcomes for Ethereum large range of factor probabilities as a result of less focused potential use case.

Investment Strategy

To consider the various analyses that we performed giving a weighting to every analysis and thereafter use this weighting to allocate the funds of the crypto portfolio. The result of the regression analysis are very positive, although we largely need to discount its result in the overall portfolio decision due to its limitations and has been given only 5% weight. As a result of the nature of the Monte Carlo analysis and it being able to incorporate a number of factors that have a potential to play out over the next five years; the remaining weight has been allocated to the result of this analysis. In addition, to increase severity, we have introduced three different sub-criteria for the result of the analysis. The first one is the comparison of each 100 simulations, which were produced to determine which blockchain technology had a higher expectation in returns. As this result shows which currency has a higher chance of return over the five-year period, a 40% weight is given in this section. To incorporate the element of risk aversion in making investment decisions, the element of investment criteria was given 25% weight. And finally, there is ensuring that the portfolio will generate a healthy expected result to enable averaging of all the expected returns to produce a probable expected return for the duration of the investment. The final result of this evaluation is given a 30% weight. The following table gives the impact of every weightings had on the portfolio.

The results indicates that Bitcoin is a better performer, nevertheless, Ethereum has proven that it warrants a position in the portfolio. After considering everything, investing 69% in Bitcoin and 31% in Ethereum so as to maximize returns in the next five years. Following this allocation, then we can have an expected value for this portfolio after five years as:

(1.42*0.69) + (1.20*0.31)* $1 *million* = $1,351,800

In A Nutshell

With the arrival of blockchain technology as it is, forecasting a five-year increase in the value of either Ethereum or Bitcoin needs a lot of factors to be considered. By combining linear regression, qualitative research through interviews with industry experts and Monte Carlo analysis, we can make a conclusion that Ethereum having a lower expected value has a greater variance due to strong correlation with hype, news and speculation. Ethereum having a great span of outcomes, shows that it should be included in the investment portfolio in order to take advantage of this fact. On the other hand, Bitcoin can leverage its existing user base and is very likely to experience much growth in five years' time.

Trading With Monero

Monero has experienced a thrust with the recent adoption by Oasis darknet markets and Alphabay. This has resulted in price explosion. Monero is the market preferred anonymity focused cryptocurrency. The rise of Monero has rather been slow until August 2016 when it started to rise. It has endlessly competed fueled by speculation and hype rather than utility and innovation. The developers and community of Monero focused on the upgrading and perfecting code to guarantee reliable anonymity. They paid little attention to cosmetic factors. This resulted to Monero remaining undervalued and unnoticed. Overshadowed by ethically unquestionable and less technically impressive cryptocurrencies. Across social media, forums and other venues of the same where coins received pumping, Monero was hardly mentioned and was severally dismissed as a boring coin.

Through the merits of its code, it won the trust of many people. It has gradually acquired the reputation for competence and reliability. Monero is distinct from the majority of altcoins as it was not cloned from Bitcoin codebase. Monero was introduced as a folk of Bytecoin. The anonymity properties of Monero makes it an excellent choice for darknet market trade and other privacy-sensitive applications.

Monero's price surge and bust and broader market recognition was as a result of it hitting a couple of darknet markets. The acceptance of Monero by such large markets was not a big deal, rather it reflects a growing trust among those whose freedom rely upon anonymity. For someone who is entirely new in cryptocurrency, there is a lot to learn before making any major investment into Monero. Start with cryptographic techniques that underpin Bitcoin and study the functions of its blockchain. Do not skip the Bitcoin learning part, despite the fact that your main interest is Monero. With no reference to Bitcoin, you cannot be able to properly, predict the relative weakness and strength of Monero.

Chapter 7: Cryptocurrency Fundamental Analysis And Ico Checklist

Before taking a position when dealing with analysis for trading a cryptocurrency on fundamental basis consider the following:

How Active Is The Development

An active cryptocurrency Github is able to give you information on, what is going on with projects and the exact features that are being implemented. Know the commits and mergers that have been recently conducted. For a more active commits, makes a token to be priced more than 10 million USD.

How Active Is The Main Developer

The involvement of the developer determines the value of a token. When a developer or a community is engaged with a token, it will have a higher chance of volume and potential chance for a trade.

Characteristics Of A Coin

1) Are there investors who are looking to exit when the token is trading on a market?
2) What is the distribution of the coin?
3) What is the current float
4) Is the coin a clone of Litecoin, Ethereum or Bitcoin? If so, does it have any noticeable features for the token to have value?

We will look at the importance of performing a fundamental analysis for cryptocurrencies. Plus how to have your own diligence before you can invest. The world of cryptos can be very intimidating due to the use of computer language and the technical concept. With the addition of inefficiency of resources to help you.

Importance Of Performing Your Own Analysis

Cryptocurrencies do not have any financial statements, making it radically different to perform a fundamental analysis. This is because:

- Cryptocurrencies are in developmental stages as the cryptos space is in an infant stage. Therefore this means there are in limited uses in the real world hence, the lack of records to show.

- Cryptocurrencies represents assets in a network. Its sustainability is not centered in revenue generation but it is dependent on the participation of the community.

As a result, a different methodology is used when performing a fundamental analysis on crypto. It is important to assess the capability plus the potential of coins. Therefore, the need of research. This is also important because of the complex nature and underlying technology of cryptos.

Understanding coins fundamentals ensures that you make informed investments decisions. Plus keeping you in loop of things, having your own opinion and stand in the crypto world.

ICO Checklist

ICO, which means Initial Coin Offering, is where tokens are created and sold to the public. You will get a cryptographic token in wallet software, where its value is determined by the economy created by the entity.

You need to know where to get key information when it comes to assessing a coin. Below are sources where you can get the information:

1. Coin's White Paper

The developmental team is to provide a detailed proposal that outlines the mechanics and purpose of the coin. This is the main source of assessing the fundamentals of a coin. Ensure that you read the coin's white paper before you invest. The disadvantage is it can get technical due to the technical language plus concepts used.

2. Coin's Slack Channel Or Blog

This is the main avenue of communication for the core developmental team. By joining their channel you are able to view their interactions with the community. Asking questions will enable you to get more information on the coin. You can also follow their updates on official blogs.

3. Community Forums

Forums give you a chance to understand the coins plus the sentiments behind them. You can be able to grasp the mechanics of a coin, through the diversity of thought the community forum will offer. As it's well informed.

Here is a checklist to help you find a good ICO to invest in:

- The business plan after the ICO, this is because many ICO's don't have this.
- Do they have a good and experienced developer plus marketing team?
- What are they offering? Make sure you pay attention to the concept of ICO even if you don't understand.
- Check their website, access their business model, read their white paper, for experienced developers are transparent
- Know how many outlets they are part of
- The support of the community
- Do they have an ICO member on LinkedIn as this helps a user to see the experience of an individual?

- The company must have a road map and it's full financial plan
- The company needs to have a communication department that works well so that an investor is able to ask questions.
- The company should have a realistic vision
- Funds are escrowed
- Rules, laws and regulations governing the company
- A detailed white paper

There are so many ICO's which SCAM. SCAM ICOs don't want to spend money on social media, marketing or even answer users question for they are here to rip people of their money. Also scammers do not know concepts behind ICO and they prefer to hide from smart investors. Look for the above things when choosing an ICO website to invest in and avoid companies with:

- Bad language as they use speculative language or encourage you on fear of missing out.
- Poor assets, they have shallow websites as they are trying to be as anonymous as possible.

Investing In Profitable ICOs

In 2013, the first ICO campaign by Omni Layer took place. Since then there has been a rise in the investment of free crowdfunding events. ICO products have been out in the internet market for the last two years, having increasingly huge amounts of token sales able to break boundaries of $3,33,094,276 USD. This has resulted to early investors in Bitcoin cryptocurrencies earning over 3,000%.

Investing in ICOs comes with risks which are important for you to understand, but there is no need of overthinking about them. When it comes to choosing which ICOs to invest in, it's important for you to understand the team, the whitepaper and the product offering plus everything there is about the ICO.

When you receive your token, trade them for other cryptocurrencies like ETH, BTC or EDU. You can sell 30% and keep 70% of your tokens. Use the 30% to begin to earn back your investment. Dealing with tokens posts a lot of fear and uncertainties do not let this discourage you.

Tokens and cryptocurrencies are dependent on the market activity, as they can either appreciate or depreciate just like any other store of value. Over the years the value of BTC has risen over its contemporaries. Its value was originally $0.008, in a period of seven years its value has rose to $6,000. While investing in ICO its profit can be divided into two:

1. Short Term

Here tokens are bought during main sale or presale or after the token are listed in the exchange market. Quick profits are made as they are sold. This allows investors to purchase token at a cheaper rate if they did not get in early on the period of token sales.

2. Long Term

In other cases investors keep their tokens for a long period, waiting for the full measure of the tokens to be attained. This kind of investors gains from day to day trading activities. People with speculative feeling tend to have optimistic returns gain on merit.

As an investor before choosing an ICO to invest in, consider the following:

- The quality of the project. Check to see if their social media is inflated.
- Presence of a well-defined road map.
- Celebrity endorsements available and it should not be a distraction from the real product.
- The integrity of their profile and development team. Ensure there is a track record of the business and team.

It's important to note that you ought not to invest due to fear of missing out, instead due to investment purposes which is reached at through informed decisions.

List of ICOs Resources

For those who want to launch, track or research on initial coin offerings here is a list of web resources.

Coin Schedule

All the ICOs, milestones, events related to altcoins and Bitcoin and crowdfunding are listed. The dates used are from different sources which includes: slack channels, forums, newsletters and official coin websites among others. The lists are organized by coin, date and tittle. They are usually updated weekly and at times more than once in a day.

Here projects that are considered worth following and investing in are listed, which consists of best projects plus ICO crowdfunding. Coinschedule is a resource you can use to keep bookmarked.

Cryptocompare

The latest crypto trends are discussed as cryptocompare offers a platform for discussions and monitoring of markets. Cryptocompare offers accurate price dynamics plus market volume data as from 25 top crypto exchanges which includes: Ethereum, Litecoin and Bitcoin among others. Not only cryptocompare monitors raw market but it also produces a plethora of analytical editorials which includes: reviews, guides, top lists of cryptocurrencies and businesses.

It's a website that offers its visitors the chance to engage and contribute to conversation as it's a social platform. There is also a portfolio feature that allows, the user to monitor their own holdings using a base currency which they prefer. Users are also able to monitor their exposure in various platforms whether or not they are exchanges or wallets.

Ambisafe

Using Ambisafe a user can issue assets, sell the assets to other users plus allowing users to store and trade assets. You can create the tokens in two different ways which includes:

- Issuing more tokens than what can be sold then an ICO destroys the rest. This method is used by Taas.
- You can also collect investments, issue tokens to correspond the amount of investments. Chronobank and Waves uses this.

The second case can be used if you are using the Ambisafe Investor's Wallet in collecting investments. The first case enables the selling of your assets to the participating cryptocurrency exchanges. This is beneficial to your investors, for they are able to use familiar trading websites for them, to purchase ICO tokens.

When investments are made using the Ambisafe Wallet and partner exchanges follow the steps below:

Step One

Issuing assets to be purchased by investors through, registering at Ambisafe website and Master Wallet. In this stage you are an owner of the tokens. Add two owners or more and insist on two confirmations for an operation in Master Wallet. This prevents lockout cases in case an owner loses the account password. Each password has to be securely stored.

Step Two

Purchase a license for your Ambisafe Investor's Wallet, which is a web application that is written in Django and Python. Ambisafe offers customization, branding plus a secure server configuration. For the wallet to function it requires:

- Ambisafe keystore SaaS subscription which stores encrypted Ethereum account containers with a high reliability. Loss of the containers can lead no control of the purchased assets.
- MySQL or PostgreSQL database for storing rest of the wallet data.
- Ambisafe Keyserver SaaS subscription to accept Bitcoin as the payment method.
- Ambisafe Supernode SaaS subscription for communication with Ethereum blockchain.

When you are done with the installation and the login of the wallet panel admin, the address of the token will be seen. The wallet backend controls the address. It's this address that allows users to get the assets purchased during ICO. Using the Master Wallet send a supply of token to the address.

At this particular stage you will be able to logout, purchase your assets and register a test account in your wallet. Therefore, Ambisafe ensures everything works plus looks good before your wallet starts production and ICO.

Step Three

At this stage there are negotiations with the exchanges in order to add your asset to the supported list. You should be able to send reserve of tokens to your deposit exchange address for the users to purchase them during ICO.

Step Four

When ICO is over, destroy the non-purchased tokens by withdrawing from your Master Wallet cold storage address plus employing the revoke command.

Other ICO resources includes: Smith+ Crown, ICOO, ICO Staker, TokenMarket, ICO Alert, ICO Bench, Applancer and Bl4nkcode among others.

Conclusion

Money transactions between companies or individuals is mostly centralized and regulated by a third party. Making currency transfer or digital payment to require a credit card provider or bank to act as a middleman in completing the transaction. In this case, a fee is charged by a credit card or a bank company for the transaction. Thereby centralizing the transaction system, and all information and data are controlled and managed by a third party, and not the 2 main entities that are involved in the currency transaction. Development of cryptocurrency has solved this problem. The main aim of cryptocurrency is creating a decentralized setting/environment where there is no third party controlling data and transactions.

Current Applications Of Cryptocurrency Technology

- ➢ Blockchain's first application in Bitcoin is as a new way of making payments.

- Beyond Bitcoin, the blockchain application as settlement and payment mechanism is in banking, where reconciliations of records that relate to transactions between different banks can be time consuming and costly consuming when it used to be performed through traditional channels.

- Non-financial applications opportunities are endless.

- **For Anti-Counterfeit Solution**: BlockVerify uses this technology providing blockchain based anti-counterfeit clarifications, hence introducing transparency in supply chains. It's mostly used in luxury items, electronics, diamonds and pharmaceutical industries.

- **Filament**: a startup, which provides a decentralized Internet of Things (IoT) software stack where it uses bitcoin blockchain to allow gadgets to store unique identities on the public ledger.

Future Applications Of Cryptocurrency

- In future Blockchain technology can be used to track the unique history of people's devices, this will be through recording ledger of data/information exchanges between web services, it and other devices, and human users.

- Blockchains could also enable several smart devices to be independent agents, by autonomously conducting a range of transactions.

- **Distributed cloud storage**: in the next 3 to 5 years, Blockchain data storage is expected to become a massive disruptor. Especially since current cloud storage services are centralized.

- **Digital identity**: people will not need to worry anymore about their digital security. This is because Blockchain technologies will make managing and tracking digital identities both efficient and secure, resulting in reduced fraud and seamless sign-on.

- **Smart contracts:** soon legally binding programmable digitized contracts is to be enrolled in the blockchain

- **Digital voting**: one of the greatest obstacle of getting electoral processes online, is security. However, with blockchain, one can check that his/her vote was transmitted successfully while remaining anonymous.

Enthusiasts, investors, consumers, or even tech-savvy geeks may be good Bitcoin buffs. All this type of people may follow every bit of cryptocurrency news and have one question in their mind. Individuals may want to find out if the optimistic future can be carved out of investing in different cryptocurrencies. Well, it is not a startling or gimmick infomercial. Investing in cryptocurrency can be an intelligent attempt, apart from being lucrative. The latest popularity of Cryptocurrency market can't be denied. The boom of bitcoin in 2013 together with its enormous increase in value resulted to its reputation. The roller coaster ride of cryptocurrencies known as Altcoins and Bitcoin got a place of distinction in each dictionary found in the world. These digital currencies over the years have earned sufficient exposure, and a career involved in investing in them can provide income. However, the investors should have three main things – some money, ample time, and an undying perseverance.